I0815780

# Creative Homes

Interiors and Design in Belgium

gestalten

# The Manifold Beauty of Belgian Interiors

In celebrating 21 perspectives on living through distinct Belgian residences, *Creative Homes* captures the spirit of Belgitude—in spaces shaped by intuition, materiality, and the blur between life, work, and play.

Modest in size, surrounded by larger, louder neighbors, Belgium has always defied easy definition. Its cultural output—art, design, architecture—is both vast and distinctive, and reveals a country that speaks softly yet unmistakably shapes the conversation. From the surrealism of René Magritte to the rustic charm of Axel Vervoordt's interiors, Belgian design continues to spark international admiration. Compared to the design waves of fellow continentals—think Danish modernism or Milanese Memphis—Belgians lean into the slow burn. Less flashy, more enduring; no crescendo, but rather a continuum of quality. Precisely that subtlety is what makes Belgian interiors all the more intriguing and, perhaps, desirable. They have become synonymous with quiet, understated sophistication: minimal yet warm, conceptual yet sensory, with a deep respect for materials and craft. Belgian design has not evolved in a vacuum, however, and remains in constant motion. The imprint of bordering countries is traceable through distinct style cues—from Bauhaus functionalism to the geometric flair of Dutch de Stijl and the chic elegance of art deco. Global undercurrents ripple through as well, from post-digital fatigue and the urge to soothe the nervous system, to a growing consciousness around sustainable living.

*Creative Homes* presents a vivid panorama of contemporary Belgian domestic culture, tracing how remarkable houses give shape to the ways in which Belgians live, create, and connect in space.

With 21 homes portrayed through intimate narrative and the crisp lens of Luc Roymans, *Creative Homes: Interiors and Design in Belgium* places a contemporary thermometer in the heart of Belgian domestic culture. This book reveals the stories behind remarkable spaces and the equally remarkable people who designed and inhabit them—offering insight into their process and boundless inspiration. With the turn of each page, you are swept into the rich diversity of a nation whose accommodations span narrow city streets and green, rolling hills. Peeking into the residences of multidisciplinary creatives and curious scientists, of publishers and fashion designers, each dwelling strikes a unique chord. Take Tom Callebaut's G-LAB (p. 90)—transformed from a traditional family home into a co-living experiment for the future, with literal open doors and born out of unfiltered optimism and empathy. That same yearning for openness—rooms that are fluid, not fixed; a layout that allows both autonomy and connection—is mirrored in the home of Caroline De Malsche and Jurgen Maelfeyt (p. 80). Spaces are less delineated, designed for freer, more open living, and there is a plea for a spatial logic that guides circulation, allowing daily life to unfold effortlessly around it. Casa UMU (p. 202), once a farmhouse, goes one step further, merging this sense of connectivity with a still, nature-bound spirituality.

The countryside as an arena, in one form or another, resurfaces time and again throughout other featured residences. Think of Yusuf Yaman's old cow stable (p. 188) or Annick Van De Weghe's former horse barn (p. 138): both repurposed for living, yet never erasing what once was. These two houses embrace a charming clash between Belgian minimalism and expressive maximalism in a way that feels homey—think shabby chic. In both, white floors, beams, and ceilings set a clean tone, just as it does in the house of architect Katrien Van Goethem (p. 24), where, on the contrary, the decor leans toward quiet, uncluttered simplicity. There may be few objects in sight, but every one of them is intentional. That same pared-back approach is apparent in the spaces designed by KAAI 7 (p. 34), TENARCHITECTS (p. 12), and Blauwberg (p. 72)—the last two also infusing a hint of Japandi. Composed and deeply peaceful, they still manage to hold warmth and individuality in every carefully placed item—from self-made art to timeworn mementos, salvaged finds, and vintage items.

*Creative Homes* reveals how the Belgian approach to living—sensitive, refined, ever-evolving—offers not just aesthetic inspiration but a lens for future ways of inhabiting and making a home.

In a post-Covid world, the Belgian home is more hybrid than ever. Once just a place to eat, sleep, and seek shelter, the Belgian home has become a true shape-shifter, morphing into a gallery, a listening lounge, or an office as daily life demands. It sometimes even functions as a coworking hub with a touch of hospitality, as in the home of Femke Vandevelde and Jens Govaert (p. 124), or a world of wonder for children's workshops, designed for endless creative play, as in Tinne Moorthamer and Geoffrey Schampaert's spacious abode (p. 12). The move to soften the threshold between interior and landscape—through lush indoor greenery and windows that frame the outdoors—taps into biophilic design thinking, which seeks to deepen our connection with nature. Just look at the property of Antoine Vandewoude (p. 148), bursting with flora, inside and out, or Mieke Berendsen's bungalow (p. 178) where the rear facade seems to dissolve entirely, letting the lawn spill inward.
What truly defines Belgian homes today? Considered choices, clever reinventions, and an effortless dialogue between past, present, and beyond. They are rarely overdesigned or static; they allow room for evolution and personal expression. These are not simply interiors—they are fragments of lives, glimpses into the private logic of those who reside in them. Together, they form a living portrait of what Belgitude looks like today, brick by brick: thoughtful, tactile, layered, and astonishingly diverse.

*— Sanne Bolten*

Remote Bungalow, Brasschaat. *Designed by* TENARCHITECTS.
*Inhabited by* Tinne Moorthamer, Geoffrey Schampaert, and children

# Serene Earthy Sanctuary

Half embraced by dense woodland, half outlined by a reflective pond—this home is enchantingly framed by the elements. Though the structure's sharp angles and geometric lines reflect Bauhaus, the heavy brown brick and roof tiles help it settle into the landscape, if not vanish into it. Before moving into this expansive retreat in the woods, residents Tinne Moorthamer and Geoffrey Schampaert spent two decades floating on water. As former inland shippers, they had one certainty: when moving ashore, they would take the calm and sensory life of the waves with them. Their briefing for TENARCHITECTS was clear—nature had to take the lead. Originally designed and built by a technical draftsman in the 1970s, the bungalow was reimagined for the couple and their kids as they entered this new chapter in their lives. Extra-large expanses of glass dissolve the line between indoors and out, letting the environment flow freely inside. Fully collapsible accordion windows in the kitchen amplify the open-air feel, with robins and foxes occasionally peeking in to satisfy their curiosity. Inside, the color palette unfolds in nuanced earthy shades, from rich browns to layered greens, reflecting the tones of the surrounding nature. Spanning 3,120 sq. ft. (290 m$^2$), this home is a study in balance, where Belgian minimalism and Japandi principles merge, and spatial fluidity defines each room. Rustic accents bring warmth, from the towering wooden sculpture to the display of dried giant hogweed blooms. Serax papier-mâché pots and Herman Miller polyester chairs introduce a modern contrast, while artworks, travel souvenirs, pebbles, and seashells add a personal touch. Expected or impromptu, there is always room for dinner guests at the iconic marble-topped Tulip table, designed by Saarinen for Knoll. The one thing that instantly draws the eye upon entering? The sunken seating area, lined with a built-in bench and a plush, high-pile rug—a wink to the coziness of a ship's cabin, but above all, a beautiful homage to the family's maritime past.

WOLVENKINDEREN

Brushed-gold accents lend a refined touch to the freestanding bathtub, against the backdrop of a distinctly 1970s glass-block wall. The children's room, decorated with scientific illustrations, suggests a little scientist in the making sleeps there.

ik heb het
nog nooit
gedaan dus
ik denk dat ik
het wel kan
-Pippi Langkous-
H2SO4
SO3H
E=mc2
mixture
catalysts
CO
C+O2
H2O
OH

Lofty Cocoon, Antwerp. *Designed and inhabited by* Katrien Van Goethem

# Layers of Stillness

For Katrien Van Goethem, the blueprint for a distraction-free refuge and an uncompromising way of living took shape in the wake of a breakup and a move to Antwerp's city center—a new chapter free from noise, shaped by intention. Set within the former warehouse of the Roode Pelikaan coffee roastery, Van Goethem's loft began as nothing more than four structural columns. An architect by training, she crafted every detail: the bed, the kitchen island, the cabinetry, and the lounge area. With ceilings soaring higher than 13 ft. (4 m), Van Goethem saw an opportunity to experiment with levels, turning the house into a layered composition. The cut-out spaces and box-in-box concept were inspired by Michael Heizer's *North, East, South, West*—a work she has long admired and now, in a way, finds herself living within. Seeking a deeper sense of presence, the architect anchored herself in the timeless appeal of the conversation pit. Seating areas for intimate discussion have been around for ages, peaking in mid-century Europe and America between the 1950s and 1970s. Van Goethem's approach reinterprets a semi-conversation pit, where a gentle curvature shapes the space. A slight elevation in the sunken lounge forms the seating area, facing large windows delicately veiled in sheer, pleated curtains for privacy. The chalk-white poured floor, minimalist kitchen, and brick walls create a sense of openness while instilling a calming clarity. Color finds its place here too, through vibrant primary accents—plush sofa cushions and a Calder-inspired installation, commanding attention in their own subtle yet striking way. The untouched support beams retain their aged chocolate-brown hue. That raw, unfinished wood and natural texture is distinctly Belgian, yet the ultra-minimalist execution leans toward the futuristic. With its fluid form and brushed-steel finish, the kitchen island reads as much as a sculptural artwork as a functional element.

The stainless-steel kitchen island doubles as a sink, cooking station, and impromptu bar. The circular shower, with its slick, sci-fi feel, looks ready to beam you into another dimension—proof that daily routines do not have to be ordinary.

The sleek bed with headboard is made of ALPI Sottsass Grey veneer. A cutesy drinks' trolley repurposed for kitchen staples, a floral arrangement, and two chairs create a cheerful scarlet-red trio.

Former Dentist's Office, Kortrijk. *Designed by* Jan Lefevere/KAAI 7.
*Inhabited by* Jan Lefevere and Griet Vandermeersch

# Oxygen and Light

This is a home with a striking void in the ceiling, stretching upward like a light-filled shaft. It feels almost otherworldly—and with the way it catches light, it truly is. Given that this was once a dentist's office, it is hard to ignore the irony of such a prominent cavity. The space, dating back to 1962 and at one time serving as a warehouse, sat untouched for more than two decades before Jan Lefevere and Griet Vandermeersch took it under their wing. Together, the couple juggles three jobs and three children in a bustling city. Needless to say, their craving for calm was understandable. So, rather than having a spare room, they chose to carve out this light-filled crater, drawing brightness into the heart of their home—the kitchen. Creeping plants cascade gracefully into the space, their green leaves flowing downward. The garden, lush and abundant, feels like a natural extension of the kitchen and living area, seamlessly linked by a large sliding-glass wall. Lefevere, an architect by profession, came across the property through a client and immediately saw potential despite its dark and confined feel at the time. The shed at the back, accessible through the garden, caught Vandermeersch's eye in particular—it now houses her collection of vintage finds gathered over the years. He is the aesthetic thinker; she is the practical one. Inspired by architect Juliaan Lampens, Jan chose to embrace similar brutalist references in his Kortrijk home. The tension between wood and concrete resulted in a space that is both sculptural and grounded, where materiality defines atmosphere. The same interplay extends to the furnishings: white Bertoia side chairs by Knoll, with their steel-wire frames, contrast with the soft, curvy forms of a gray Togo sofa set by Michel Ducaroy for Ligne Roset. Despite the minimalist approach to the interior, it never feels stark, thanks to colorful accents and personal touches—a wooden children's bike, framed photos, coffee-table books. This is a perfect marriage between Belgian austerity and warmth, where raw materials meet thoughtful details, adding depth and personality to the space.

The wooden seating, designed in a semicircle, was created by Lefevere himself. The marble side table in the living room is a Saarinen classic. A vibrant bike swing in kelly green invites motion—and never fails to set the room in playful action.

The vintage cerulean sink in the bathroom is a unique find by Vandermeersch, while the matching floor, inspired by the bar at Budascoop in Kortrijk, was selected by Lefevere. Earthy dried flowers mimic the tones of frames, beams, and even clustered coats.

Artist Oasis, Ghent. *Designed by* Maria Scarpulla. *Inhabited by* Maria Scarpulla, Jori Hernalsteen, and children

# Home in Full Color

Sometimes, the next home is right under your nose—something Maria Scarpulla and her partner, Jori Hernalsteen, experienced firsthand. A designer and painter, Scarpulla had a furniture studio that was mere steps from the old textile factory that would become their new house. The space had just been renovated, allowing her and Hernalsteen to settle in immediately. And with 2,500 sq. ft. (235 $m^2$) of living space and a 1,350 sq. ft. (125 $m^2$) garden, there is no shortage of room. A peaceful oasis, the place has the added perk that the factory gates close on weekends—perfect for children playing outside. Despite adjustments needed to make the house move-in ready, many original details remain intact—patinated wooden floors and support beams, retro tile patterns in the hallway, and gently curved ceilings. In the living room, the original terracotta stone floor sets the tone. Its weathered hues form a natural palette, serving as the space's defining element. The pink and red dinner table, an original Scarpulla, is crafted from lacquered steel and sustainable MDF. Around it sits a lively mix of purposefully mismatched chairs: a Bertoia wire chair, a Wegner Wishbone, and various school chairs. The discreet reading nook in the corner is strategically placed next to two bookshelves, perfect for curling up with a cup of coffee or tea. There, colorful coffee-table books mingle with amusing curios that include vintage barber heads and delicate bird figurines. The interior breathes eclecticism, the sum of Scarpulla's worldly roots and her design practice. Raised in the green hills and yellow tones of Umbria, in Italy, she grew attuned to the world through sensory experiences. The daughter of an artist, she carries the imprint of those landscapes and their architecture with her. She refines form and function by questioning them, allowing them to transcend their conventional purpose. Whether in painting or design, Scarpulla masterfully fuses Belgian simplicity with southern flair.

The L-shaped, wooden-topped, black kitchen block lets colors pop—especially the Kazimir Malevich-like framed work with minimalist flair. The red Berber rug injects a kaleidoscopic presence and contrast into a space already rich in layers and texture.

GROTE FOTOGRAFEN

A loft
111-5

Former Bank Branch, Zwijnaarde. *Designed by* Philippe De Berlangeer, GAFPA.
*Inhabited by* Bart De Bock, Deborah Rochtus, and children

# Colorful Concrete Vault

While others might fantasize about breaking into a bank, computer programmer Bart De Bock and business controller Deborah Rochtus did the exact opposite—they locked themselves inside one. Not literally, of course, but close enough, as they have made a former bank their home. Looking for a spacious ground-floor apartment near Ghent, the couple were on the point of giving up when an unexpected online ad changed everything. A vacant former bank, still cluttered with office gates, a cash machine, and an armored door, stopped them in their tracks. With the apartment above also for sale, they gained twice the space: truly a high-interest investment. Turning the place into a child-friendly home was no small feat, but architect Philippe De Berlangeer of architecture firm GAFPA was up for it. A specialized company helped to cut through the wall and ceiling—without it, the vault was inaccessible; the scene could have been pulled from a heist film. Since the building was originally a residence before its 1980s conversion into a bank, traces of its domestic past remained, informing its new layout. While preserving office-like details, the ground floor was structured into three long, imaginary strips extending toward the street. Tall, frosted-glass doors with ceiling-level windows mark the transition into the private areas. By mirroring the concrete bunker into a symmetrical glass volume, a passage was created between the living room and kitchen. Beyond functional, it was designed around shared moments with friends and family—talking, sipping, staying close. The patio enhances transparency, making the full depth of the home tangible. Inside, colors and wood details playfully interact against a cloudy gray cement floor. An enormous, coral velvet sofa steals the spotlight, while pre-loved wooden crates find new purpose as a TV stand and record storage. A green spiral staircase playfully invites you to climb it, while houseplants add a concrete jungle feel. Eschewing excess, the couple favors Belgian restraint, letting materials speak for themselves. Since moving in, they have resisted buying more furniture, choosing instead to appreciate the treasures already at hand.

The custom-made, light-wood kitchen island, made for gathering, doubles as a bar, mini-library, and toy car display. The vintage teak wall unit proves that not just objects, but even headwear, deserve to be proudly on show.

The vintage black-and-white twin credenza, semi-stacked atop one another, creates an optical illusion. Thanks to a yellow Moccamaster and a silver percolator, specialty coffee is always within reach in this home.

Reclaimed Shell, Antwerp. *Designed and inhabited by* Heidi Veeckmans

# The Quiet Factory

Modern cities do not just grow—they roar. With honking traffic, swelling crowds, and clamoring facades, silence has become a rare luxury, nearly impossible to find. But architect Heidi Veeckmans has carved out her own slice of heaven in a former Antwerp factory—once raw-edged, now deeply personal. With dedication and inventiveness, she repurposed the plant into a soft-spoken loft, a tranquil two-person bubble for herself and her daughter, Emmylou. Upon experiencing the space for the first time, it was the light that drew Veeckmans in. She bought the property as an empty shell, letting its particular brightness steer the redesign. But one design dilemma loomed: how do you reimagine a 33-foot-long (10-meter-long) void into a home that keeps the airy loft feel without sacrificing privacy? Leave it to Veeckmans, seasoned architect at Stramien cv and tireless hands-on maker, to solve the puzzle with precision. To preserve the open space while creating intimacy where preferred, she devised a wooden volume with a bathroom, laundry storage, and a tucked-away sleeping nook for Emmylou. Keeping views unobstructed—and costs down—was key from the start. There is no disguising the building's foundation—unfinished concrete ceilings, stark support columns, and a gray screed floor form a continuous, textural base that gives the loft its unmistakably industrial character. Veeckmans enjoys creating wonder with limited means—proof that beauty lies in the small things. The house is filled with repurposed furniture, IKEA staples, and secondhand scores—lifted by her own art, macramé planters, and a unique collection of foraged finds. Emmylou makes her mark too, hanging feathers and twigs in her alcove or transforming sticks into sculptures. To temper the omnipresent grays, Veeckmans leaned into earthy hues and natural textures—thereby balancing the grayscape of each room. It is Belgian minimalism, reimagined: raw, resourceful, and full of heart.

The minimalist island may look custom and straight out of a magazine, but it is actually a clever IKEA hack—two rows of standard cabinet units finished with a white laminate countertop. The dreamy paintings, inspired by her time in Montana across the pond, are Veeckmans's own.

Veeckmans's favorite perch? The terrace. Built-ins below the window double as seating and storage, making the most of every inch. Glossy white tiles offer a nod to retro, while exposed OSB panels add a utilitarian touch.

KOFFIE
STORIES

Multifunctional Row House, Meise. *Designed by* Blauwberg.
*Inhabited by* Mark Verdoodt, Barbara Puttemans, and son

# Mini Minimalist Chameleon

Resident Mark Verdoodt calls it a hobby that spiraled—his modest row house, now a fully realized multiuse family home. Originally part of a large farm in the Halle-Vilvoorde district of Flemish Brabant, it was later split into three separate homes. Though the transformation is striking, the original doorposts remain, offering a quiet clue to the building's history as a former stable. As the cofounder of a company specializing in bespoke woodworking, Verdoodt knows the art of custom craftsmanship inside and out. The ingenuity behind every element reveals just how freely he let his imagination run in this home makeover. A house in flux, it shifts with the seasons: an indoor barbecue morphs into a winter fireplace, while a floating terrace seamlessly transforms into a private pool. Verdoodt did not let square footage limit his vision—his experimental testing ground has the versatility of a luxury resort. This adaptability makes minimalism an absolute necessity, as every room is designed to transform in an instant. The living space functions as a kitchen, workspace, coffee bar, lounge, party venue, and even a fitness room. Without fixed furniture, mobile cabinets allow for a constantly evolving setup, making it possible to host dinner parties of up to 16 guests. It is almost unbelievable that this multidimensional residence spans less than 1,000 square feet (100 square meters), yet it does. There is an effortless ease to the space, reflected in the pared-down materials and objects, which are distinctly Belgian in sensibility. Mahogany wood offsets the rawness of concrete, keeping the design from feeling austere and blending Japanese simplicity with Scandi finesse. Meanwhile, framed art and carefully arranged coffee-table books inject personality without disrupting the home's crisp, uncluttered feel. Even the family's cat—a seal point Birman—looks as if it was made for this interior. The home's showstopper? A rooftop terrace, its iron framework resembling a birdcage from the street.

Concealed behind built-in cupboards lie the dressing room and an extra bathroom, while the central space doubles as a yoga studio. The kitchen opens at the touch of a remote. Three bistro tables with adjustable tops convert into a long dining table.

Lofty Layers, Ghent. *Designed by* Kristoffel Boghaert, AKB_architectuur.
*Inhabited by* Caroline De Malsche, Jurgen Maelfeyt, and children

# A Family Affair

A single look said it all. Fifteen minutes later, the decision was made—art book publishers Caroline De Malsche and Jurgen Maelfeyt were sold. The vacant beer-bottling plant in the Dampoortwijk district of Ghent, collecting dust for half a century, had cast a spell on them. Still, it took them a year to muster the strength to tell their parents, afraid they had gotten in over their heads. In retrospect, they were—but determination prevailed. With AKB architect Kristoffel Boghaert's vision, they created a lofty yet familial triplex, as tastefully layered and playful as a parfait: a residence annexed to an art bookshop/gallery. After detailed discussions with the couple, Boghaert decided to reject traditional layouts and designed the house around the family's needs. While some Belgian homes lean into structured zoning and a sense of enclosure, this one embraces fluidity. Multilayered and magnetic, the living room anchors the space, with intentionally modest bedrooms extending from its core—a conscious design choice that encourages organic movement between shared and private spaces. A dark, cloudlike concrete floor, white bathroom tiles, and light-teal bedroom flooring bring a crisp balance to the natural warmth of the wood. This makes the perfect backdrop for tantalizing works by artists such as Max Pinckers, Tom Callemin, and Hana Miletić—carefully chosen by the couple, whose expertise as art book publishers has sharpened their eye for visual clarity. The joinery, made from pine and birch plywood, extends into a kitchen island crafted from a dark-green concrete variant. Serene materials, favored by both Boghaert and the couple, hint at understated Scandi elegance. An abundance of windows floods the home with natural light from sunrise to sunset. The spacious garden has multiple access points, designed not merely as architectural features but as thoughtful gestures toward daily ease and flow. It adds generous square feet of livability and freedom—much to the residents' delight. There, a rusty Weltevree outdoor oven stands cheerfully perched, like a little guardian of the home.

JERUSALEM
PLENTY

The sleek dining table doubles as a ping-pong table, while colorful stacked crates and a toy house add lively accents. The kitchen breaks with the home's linearity, and the split-level living area amplifies its generous sense of space.

Pops of bright yellow and orange from made-to-measure curtains energize the space, while plywood panels highlight structure and depth. Light pours in year-round, keeping the space open and connected—an essential feature for De Malsche and Maelfeyt.

G-LAB, Bruges. *Designed by* TC PLUS. *Inhabited by* Tom Callebaut and family

# Rethinking Home Life

Life moves fast, cultures collide, and global connection is both exhilarating and exhausting. In this notion, interior architect Tom Callebaut found both a grounding point and an optimistic new philosophy on living. Seeing opportunity in abundance, he made a radical decision, aspiring to shape a world that is softer and more intentional. Together with his family, he transformed their home into G-LAB: a shared living space for the five of them and an open residence for curious visitors. More than a living space, it is a statement—a lead-by-example approach to communal living, challenging polarization by rolling out the red carpet for the unfamiliar. A bold gesture to the neighborhood, and a quiet challenge to policymakers: can we rethink the way we live together? A concept that strangers were quick to embrace. Since the birth of G-LAB, hundreds of guests have been drawn in—gathering for film nights, brainstorms, fundraisers, tai chi, workshops, tea ceremonies, and beyond. It is hardly surprising—the house carries a magnetic, almost unreal energy. Its bold, minimalist interior feels straight out of a film set (think: Wes Anderson-meets-Stanley Kubrick). And with as many outdoor spaces as indoor ones, the house merges architecture with nature. Sage green carries through the garden—from the patio to the wooden fence—framing a pink exterior wall so sweet even Barbie would take note. The line between public and private is not marked by walls or doors, but by a flowing curtain—shifting between division, invitation, and intrigue. Inside, a LC4 chaise longue by Le Corbusier for Cassina is angled just so, making cloud-watching a built-in part of the day. As a social laboratory and a practice ground for hospitality, the home is also an experiment that forms part of Callebaut's doctoral research on "the generous space." A lesson in Belgian hospitality and modernism, it reminds us that in even divided times, an open door is mightier than a drawn sword.

The lounge is drenched in mustard yellow: walls, floor, built-in desk, even the Togo sofa by Michel Ducaroy for Ligne Roset. A fire-engine red Eames LCW by Vitra and a yellow school chair in the white bedroom hint they might have wandered in from elsewhere.

In the crisp white kitchen, yellow and pink reappear, paired with clean steel countertops for a fresh look. After a soak in the freestanding tub, wet feet can land on a towel—or the soft sheepskin rug that adds a plush touch.

The exterior is awash in gentle, matching hues of green, covering everything from the patio floor to the garden walls, creating a deep sense of serenity and sophistication.

Tactile Treasure Chest, Ghent. *Designed by* De Clercq + Declercq.
*Inhabited by* Amaryllis Uitterlinden, Jules Debrock, and children

# Beyond Linear Design

Friendly hues, materials, and textures slalom—quite literally—through this house, where design is beyond linear and every turn holds a surprise. Lines do not just define the space, they guide you through it, like a visual game of follow-the-leader. This is no ordinary home, and it clearly has no ordinary inhabitants. A space this dynamic almost demands residents with multiple talents—and a healthy appetite for risk. Amaryllis Uitterlinden, actress and singer-songwriter, and her partner Jules Debrock, a film producer, have shaped it as freely and expressively as they live. To reinvent their residence, they turned to a duo just as fluent in adaptability: Sofie De Clercq and Katrien Declercq of De Clercq + Declercq. Known for their thoughtful new constructions and sensitive renovations, the pair brings the same care to furniture and interior design—anchored in orientation, movement, materiality, and light. A guiding arrow of pine and perforated steel steers you through the space, serving a new use in every room. Mint and peach do not shout, they lift—gentle colors that make areas feel brighter, bigger, and beautifully soft. The kitchen embraces its height shift with frivolous terrazzo and a burgundy butcher's slab, while bold textures and colors—lacquered MDF, green laminate, and plywood—keep the eye dancing, if not zigzagging. Close to the entrance a section of the perforated wall hosts coats; near the living room, the perforations hold keys or a small frame; in the cooking area, they elevate cooking oils and condiments. With endless modulations possible, this is functional, flexible, and unexpectedly fun. Hovering above the piano, a downy light fixture disguised as a cloud looks like a piece of sky that drifted in. Impossible to ignore—and just out of reach—it dares you to try and catch it. And if there is one thing it makes clear, this home proves Belgian interiors can do it all: Memphis play, Scandi ease, and a quiet cleverness that makes room for contrast without ever forcing it.

A custom-built plywood desk stretches across the room—spacious enough for a laptop, a printer, and the occasional eureka moment. A framed photo of the couple mid-kiss, surrounded by building rubble, is a romantic reminder of the past that built this present.

France
USA
South Africa
Zuid-Afrika
DONNA TARTT De verborgen GESCHIEDENIS
Alles over de liefde
JANET FITCH WITTE OLEANDER
Catherine Clement DE REIS VAN THEO
VIKRAM SETH VERWANTE STEMMEN
EDGAR ALLAN POE VERHALEN
PATTI SMITH
ZOMER HIT 2013
Tom Lanoye Het goddelijke monster

DALI
I LIKE
BIG
MUGS
MICHAEL JACKSON
A

Historic Town House, Edingen. *Designed by* AJDVIV, Jan De Vylder.
*Inhabited by* Ayco Duyster, Joachim Wemel, and children

# Time-Honored Revival

A zig follows a zag, then suddenly—an immaculate right angle. The diagonal lines in this respectfully restored multilevel house verge on the Escheresque, holding the gaze in constant fascination. There is always something new to notice in this art deco gem: an open fireplace, a slender hallway, or a half-sliced floating door. Part of the rear section, once housing a restroom and laundry, became outdoor space. The roof was removed, walls cut open, light flooded in, and the garden came into view. The faience tiles? Still very much intact, like the original windows and floor tiles. As effortlessly chic as everything looks now, the effort behind it was nothing short of colossal. Residents, radio host Ayco Duyster, game developer Joachim Wemel, and their two children lived in the basement for four years—for two of those, without a rear facade. That is commitment—something they also recognized in Jan De Vylder, the architect who helped steer the home's revival. With no standard solutions to rely on, it was all about inventive, tailor-made thinking. Years in the making, the renovation evolved gradually. In its final chapter, architect De Vylder stepped in with a daring vision that tied everything together. The hands-on execution, however, was largely thanks to Wemel, who did nearly everything himself, fueled by hours of YouTube tutorials. Untouched by former residents, the attic now crowns the home as a master bedroom—the finishing note of the transformation. In it, a vintage modular teak wall unit by Poul Cadovius for Cado blends with the warm brick wall yet adds a surprising layer of texture that offers a tactile twist. Pastel ceramic cups and teapots, neatly stacked, lend a sweet touch to the vintage sideboard—playfully accompanied by rosewood school chairs and a fluttering mobile of blue birds. A quiet plea for slow living runs throughout the home. Its slow-burn metamorphosis and art deco touches speak to Belgium's closeness to France—not just in distance, but in a shared design language that values elegance, craft, and time.

KEITH

The homeowners' allergy to hyper-clean "Dexter kitchens"—
all gloss and no soul—resulted in a far more affordable remodel.
For just a few thousand euros, they shaped a cooking area
where everything is meant to be seen, not scrubbed out of sight.

Flanked by two new triangular windows beside the chimney, the bathroom was fully redone. A double shower adds practicality, while the freestanding tub remains deliberately uncovered—an open gesture in a thoughtful space.

15th-Century Stepped-Gable Home, Ghent. *Designed by* Ellen Van Acker.
*Inhabited by* Femke Vandevelde and Jens Govaert

# Serious Bistro Vibes

If historic buildings could talk, what stories would they reveal? The walls of this 15th-century stepped-gable home in the heart of Ghent are most likely brimming with tales. With the arrival of residents Femke Vandevelde and Jens Govaert, respectively a culinary journalist and an executive, a new era for this building was set in motion. The couple took the idea of a clean slate literally and reduced each floor to a single open volume instead of divided rooms—optimizing both natural light and spatial fluidity. Architect Ellen Van Acker infused the spaces with thoughtful design, turning Vandevelde and Govaert's passion for gastronomy into a tactile, immersive interior. Nowhere is this more evident than on the lowest floor, which features a wall clad in Hungarian-pointed parquet and a bold, green-marble countertop with dramatic veining. To complete the look, custom-designed retro Winckelmans tiles bring a touch of art deco sophistication to the room, along with bespoke furniture. Ambient lighting is perfectly curated here, with modern yet industrial pendant lamps setting the mood, all controlled by sleek round Bakelite switches in black. A steel-framed divider, filled with a kaleidoscope of figured glass, marks the home's entrance. It serves as a prelude to the welcoming ground floor, designed as a coworking area, meeting room, and brainstorm library, all with the allure of a speakeasy. The second floor is home to the comfy bedroom with an exposed concrete wall and open bathroom. The living area sits one story below, where sunlight flows in and a rooftop terrace with an outdoor shower expands the space. Laid out by the crackling fireplace, a plush Berber rug invites bare feet and slow moments—whether flipping through a coffee-table book or indulging in a sweet treat. In the home of a culinary critic and an executive with bartending skills, the kitchen is always stocked, and the fridge never lacks a tempting bite—the true embodiment of Belgian joie de vivre.

KINFOLK
Kobe Desramaults

The marble coffee table and terrazzo countertops carry forward the theme of the marble bar—proof that in this home, natural stone is the preferred choice for surface materials. The steel, six-burner gas oven brings an analog touch to intuitive cooking in this space.

T
S I
E P M
U I L E

T
S I
E P M
U I L E

The glass in the made-to-measure steel divider is filled with figured glass salvaged from a cathedral, creating an interplay of light and texture. Next to the freestanding ivory-white art deco bathtub stands a milk jug—perhaps for pouring, perhaps for bathing.

Soft Baroque, Antwerp. *Designed by* Dries Otten. *Inhabited by* Dries Luyten and family

# Past Made Present

Lively Borgerhout, an Antwerp district where global energy, elegant bars, and vintage charm collide, reeled in Dries Luyten, his partner Liz, and their three children. They fell for this row house, which—behind closed doors—holds the grace of a royal residence. But this heritage home needed more than love; it needed a clear-eyed designer with guts. Dries Otten, an interior architect and furniture designer known for his color-rich world and playful joinery, had just the right eye. His no-nonsense approach, focus on simplicity, and use of clean forms brought clarity to the home's layered character, without erasing its past. Just like the neighborhood itself, Otten elevated this house to a vibrant melting pot of contrasts. Raw concrete, joint lines and all, slices through the warmth of the cognac-hued Versailles parquet in the living room. In the next room, Arne Jacobsen Butterfly chairs in a range of colors wing their way around the dining table. Jugendstil stained-glass windows, with their ribbons and dainty florals, bring a sweet softness to every room. Along with the decorative wall and ceiling flourishes they create a palette full of pastels and character. The effect is so French rococo you can almost imagine tea served with a raised pinky... until punchy postmodern touches like the geometric bookcase snap you out of it. The black wooden kitchen block is so monochrome that only the orange water jug and stainless-steel sink add a sense of depth—almost like a trompe l'oeil. The bathroom, in contrast, takes the sink setup to a whole new dimension, with burled wood cabinetry, white basins, and a schematic tiled wall. This exchange between new and old—restraint and expressiveness—is exactly what makes contemporary Belgian homes so layered. Old bones are respected, but never left untouched, allowing thoughtful interventions to add new meaning without erasing what came before.

A modular, sage-green sofa allows for unwinding in every thinkable setup. A pop of turquoise reappears in the kitchen trash can, and a round golden trolley—carrying pots and a plant—lends a hint of Hollywood Regency flair.

Electric Eclectic, Wuustwezel. *Designed by* Annick Van De Weghe.
*Inhabited by* Annick Van De Weghe and family

# Hold Your Horses

Once a stable owned by her grandfather and now a home, fashion and jewelry designer Annick Van De Weghe's Wuustwezel residence still whispers its equestrian past. Indoors, it is a feature of refined details: a leather saddle slung over a wooden beam, a Japanese-style, five-panel artwork depicting galloping horses. Outside, it is far less subtle: a brown Shetland pony might just trot by in the garden. Hardly a coincidence, as Van De Weghe spent her youth on horseback, competing at an international level in show jumping. During the transformation, she deliberately encased the house in white, from concrete floors to the walls, ceiling, and wooden posts. The result: a pristine canvas to let her signature eclectic aesthetic roam freely. Beyond the living area—naturally flowing into the kitchen and studio—the home holds space for a dressing room, a bathroom, and three inviting bedrooms. Fearless in her use of bold patterns, Van De Weghe fuses styles with effortless ease—bohemian Ibiza warmth meets Hollywood Regency elegance, much like her fashion designs mix heritage with reinvention. A towering Eiffel Tower sculpture complements a vintage brass-and-glass dining table, while retro 1970s pillows bring a playful flair to the plush Tufty-Time sectional sofa by Mario Bellini for B&B Italia. Inspired by her global travels and circularity, Van De Weghe transforms cultural touchpoints into wearable art, such as the southern African Basotho blankets that she repurposed into eye-catching "coat jackets." Each garment is unique, handcrafted in Van De Weghe's ateliers in Belgium and Italy, as are the exquisite textiles and artifacts that run like a common thread through her home's interiors. Among them, some objects remain untouchable: her grandmother's sculptural horn coffee table and a mid-century Alfred Hendrickx sideboard, timeless heirlooms in a home that is ever-evolving yet unmistakably Van De Weghe. Her home is a vibrant, expressive departure from typically muted Belgian interiors.

The
ernational
erior Design
hibition

KLIMT
LUXURY EQUESTRIAN DESIGN
RON MUECK

ART NOW!

The black Ari lounge chair by Arne Norell is a vintage find from the 1970s, while the colorful, neatly lined kaftans are from Van De Weghe's own label. In the bedroom, a soft-pink mosquito net—almost a veil—floats between framed prints and photos, both practical and poetic.

Lush Greenery, Antwerp. *Designed by* Antoine Vandewoude.
*Inhabited by* Antoine Vandewoude and family

# Handmade Family Haven

In what might be one of the narrowest facades in Antwerp, a modest double door just 6.5 ft. (2 m) wide gives nothing away, but behind it lies the verdant oasis that is the home of carpenter and furniture designer Antoine Vandewoude, his wife Ann, and their two sons. What seems like an unassuming exterior unfolds into a family home-slash-studio, where a courtyard garden overflows with bonsai trees, wisteria, and climbing roses. Finding a spacious family home with an outdoor space had been Vandewoude's dream. Long before broadband became the norm, in the early 2000s, the couple found the property through a small classified ad in a local newspaper. The same analogue spirit remains ever present in their cozy home, where tactile materials and handcrafted elements take precedence over mass-produced designs or prevailing Belgian minimalism. Natural herringbone parquet contrasts with painted wooden floors, their timeworn patina adding character. Hand-thrown vases in all shapes and sizes sit alongside vintage curios such as antique dolls and mounted butterflies in frames. Rich in character and demanding in effort, the project took seven years to complete, requiring a full demolition and rebuild. Vandewoude's approach to reconstruction was much like his ethos in furniture-making—hands-on, deeply intuitive, and with a subtle nod to the *wabi-sabi* philosophy of embracing imperfection. Handyman Vandewoude rolled up his sleeves and took on much of the work himself, leaving electrical tasks and structural finishing to professionals. A self-taught furniture maker, his expertise in woodwork proved invaluable. It is a talent that has led to high-profile commissions, including work for fashion designer Dries Van Noten, another admirer of gardens and flowers. Vandewoude and his wife make the perfect team—she sources materials and furniture, while he reworks them into something new. Take the vintage Raymond Loewy kitchen they found online: he refreshed it in mint green and replaced the countertops with steel.

The curvy sink and bath were salvaged from a house slated for demolition, while the black-and-white veined marble was a lucky find in an antique shop. Vandewoude calls the flowing paneling a key detail—one of many ways in which he makes the space his own.

N°5
CHANEL
VIANA
EAU DE COLOGNE

The Play Factory, Ghent. *Designed by* Ophélie Slimbrouck, Studio Pêche, and Charlotte Vyncke.
*Inhabited by* Elke De Vidts, Thomas Gillis, and children

# Wild Wild Warehouse

Once a milkman's home, a sewing workshop, a storage facility, and then a squat on the outskirts of Ghent, still occupied by squatters, hardly seems like a dream start. But the vast warehouse tucked behind—over 120 square meters (1,300 square feet) of possibility—quietly pulled at Studio Woop Woop owner Elke De Vidts and Thomas Gillis, who saw not what it was, but what it could become. A property that would finally allow De Vidts to act on the long-held desire to carve out a large dedicated space for her own craft atelier—something that is almost impossible to find in this region. Imagine a shell in which a home, guest quarters, and a kids' workshop all needed to coexist under one roof—quite the spatial Rubik's Cube, and one that becomes even more personal when you know the clients. For architects Ophélie Slimbrouck and Charlotte Vyncke, however, it was a no-brainer. A commitment to sustainability shaped several interior choices, integrating reused materials and recycled objects. De Vidts believes deeply that built environments shape children's well-being and their capacity to create, which is why she champions experimentation and hands-on making. So, the house was designed to nurture just that—materials that beg to be touched, an earthy base to feel safe in, and just enough room to let the imagination run free. The interior flirts with the codes of Belgian design—raw, clever, minimal—but swaps quiet elegance for playful provocation. Every detail seems designed to lift the corners of your mouth. No need to spell it out—this place is clearly the headquarters of fun. The lime-green Smeg fridge glistens like an oversized popsicle. Papier-mâché faces grin from the shelves, cleverly repurposed as scissor holders. There are winking cushions, hands that are allowed to get messy, and an extended steel sink where everything is rinsed clean, ready for the next round of creativity. The shower's full splash of hypnotic Caribbean green reappears in the steel staircases that connect to bedrooms. OSB panels play tag with vintage wooden stools and chairs—a cheerful exchange of textures and tones.

Greenery gushes from the patios connecting the studio and living space, blurring the lines between inside and out. Cone-shaped lamps in happy colors dangle from the ceiling like tiny party hats—quirky notes that make the everyday feel just a bit more festive.

Green finds its way inside the home—leafy houseplants sprout between colorful cushions and throws, making the perfect nest for a post-finger-painting nap. With its woven texture, the jute rug lends a coastal calm that quietly ties the room together.

Reimagined Architect's Abode, Bruges. *Designed by* doorzon interieurarchitecten. *Inhabited by* Eva-Maria Bogaert, Pieter Van Hoestenberghe, and children

# Loops and Layers

A 1960s architect's dwelling, reinvigorated with retro details nearly 50 years later, proves that design always finds its way back home. The original mastermind, Rik Scherpereel—who trained under radical modernist Arthur Degeyter—lived here with his family and ran his architecture firm from this building. With its bold brick form, concrete details, and steep pent roof, the house stays true to Belgian design, where materiality is honest, structure is bold, and warmth emerges through texture. Despite her love for bright tones and patterns, current resident Eva-Maria Bogaert felt an instant connection to the dark modernist structure. She and her husband, Pieter Van Hoestenberghe, came across it through his parents, and the spark was instant: they secured it before it even hit the market. As a fashion designer, artist, and ceramicist, Bogaert never shies away from color, which is evident in every corner of her ever-developing home. Muted earthy tones define the living room, punctuated by warm and cool accents, while the kitchen glows with spring green. A feast of patterns unfolds across these spaces: brick, marble tiles, wallpaper, carpet, and wooden planks all bring their own rhythm. Add an intentional mix of objects—ranging from funky to vintage—and, suddenly, cool-headed minimalism gains an unexpected dose of humor and joy. From coffee-table books to candles and "trouvailles," they are all guided by an artist's eye—chosen instinctively for their shape, color, or feel. Greenery abounds: houseplants in all kinds of pots are scattered everywhere, but never touch the floor, as if it is lava. In the living room, they find their place on a teak mid-century credenza, while mismatching stools double as pedestals. Once an architecture studio, this is now a multifunctional space ready for future intergenerational living. Solar panels, a solar boiler, and an electric car fuel the home, while homegrown fruit is preserved as jam and juice. Leftover textiles become cushions and bags. This house is a celebration of cycles, circularity, and perhaps even satisfying full circles.

Inspired by the form of an ice-cream scoop, the kitchen island and countertop by doorzon interieurarchitecten bring a bold yet fluid statement to the space. The pink lotus wallpaper climbs onto the ceiling, while party decorations—usually short-lived—seem to have claimed their spot for good.

Unexpected pops of neon yellow brighten the space—on a candle, a cushion, even a ball of yarn with knitting needles left on the sofa. But its most daring form emerges in the bathroom, where a sculptural polyester bathtub swirls into view, overlooking the sink.

Maison Mise-en-Scène, Mont-de-l'Enclus. *Designed by* Studio Okami.
*Inhabited by* Mieke Berendsen and husband

# Hide and S(l)eek

Hidden in plain sight, a near-invisible home rises from the green hills of Pays des Collines, where Mieke Berendsen and her partner Dirk reside. Overlooking the vast Hainaut valley, the building seems to dissolve into the undulating landscape of the Flemish Ardennes. Yet, once noticed, it reveals itself as something straight out of a James Bond film. After their three children left the nest, the couple felt it was time to leave their penthouse in Ghent. This region had long been their sanctuary, with a vacation home nearby, so when a plot of land became available, they jumped at the chance. The strict building regulations of the nature reserve posed hurdles, as did administrative delays—but not enough to outweigh the couple's determination to build here. Studio Okami, an Antwerp-based architecture firm, tackled the project head-on, swaying the Urban Construction department with their concept. Berendsen and her partner gave the firm virtually carte blanche, requesting only a large, loft-like space that was open, level, and multifunctional. A flat home on a steep hill? It might sound improbable to some, but for the architects, it was intentional. Taking cues from cave dwellings, they designed a two-zone structure, maximizing the building's connection to the terrain: an open-plan living space with a kitchen and workspace at the front, and a sunken section that merges with the slope. While Belgian rural homes often embrace refined modesty, this one adds cinematic framing and composition to the mix. Light-washed oak floors, ceilings, and pillars set a calm, understated backdrop. A richly textured patchwork rug adds instant coziness. The Eames lounge chair, ottoman, and binoculars further the illusion of being in a secret service agent's lair. When the summer heat rises, the stone path leads to the raised pool for a refreshing dip. And after that—cut to closing credits.

The gently white-washed bricks create a cohesive extension from inside, giving them an airy feel. The bookshelves were designed by the couple's daughter, Elisabeth. The back patio stretches long enough to serve as a runway—or a hidden summer sun spot.

Classic marble-topped Tulip side and dining tables by Saarinen introduce soft curves to the clean lines of the interior, with Jacobsen Butterfly chairs playfully encircling the latter. A hefty black steel fireplace injects a dose of brute charm into the living room.

CLUB

Farm Paradise, Temse. *Designed by* MAN Architects. *Inhabited by* Yusuf Yaman and family

# Circular Cow House

You might catch homeowner Yusuf Yaman tending to his rhubarb patch, dressed in clogs and worn-out dungarees. Hardly the image of a typical real estate developer—but Yaman is not one for convention. Eager to roll up his sleeves, his hands-on mindset extends to his philosophy on property restoration. Rather than tearing buildings down, he restores them with patience and precision. In MAN Architects, he found a like-minded partner, sharing similar principles and a willingness to take on a creative challenge. And with good reason—this was not just about personal ambition; it was a commitment to heritage. The East Flemish farm Yaman now calls home had been in the same family since the 16th century. Though the current generation had no desire for farm life, they were intent on preserving the buildings. The premises were split—an organic farmer duo maintained the communal picking garden and future animal park, while Yaman and his family moved into the former cow and horse stable. Much of the stable's original structure remains intact—a ground floor with a lofty upper level that once stored hay. A section of the hayloft was lowered, creating a suspended seating area that bridges the main floor and first level, connecting to the bedroom, bathroom, and office. In this one-of-a-kind house, Belgian rural charm meets sustainable ingenuity, with repurposed elements informing a space that honors past and present. The authentic soul of the farm is evident in almost everything—exposed brickwork, repurposed rustic wood panels, and even a cowhide rug. The outcome? A bold, playful mix of textures, materials, and colors that feels both natural and joyful. Guided by a mindset of circularity, Yaman constantly weighed whether something could be repurposed. Kitchen cupboards were built from reclaimed stones, the stable gate transformed into a dining table, and the animals' old water trough now serves as a sink. Nevertheless, the true crown jewel may be something new—the conservatory, a later addition, where the family sits down to breakfast every day.

ANDREA
VINA

In the long kitchen, original rustic elements coexist with modern materials such as the steel Hee bar stools from Hay. Once the farmhouse door opened onto the land—now it opens conversations as a dining table. Talk about a conversation piece.

The entrance hall offers a nod to the cows that once lived here—their feed troughs now serve as a shoe rack, while a wooden harrow functions as a coat rack. The pitch-black bathroom calms the senses, with wooden touches adding quiet depth.

ANDREA

ANDREA

Casa UMU, Eksaarde. *Designed by* Sven Bullaert. *Inhabited by* Sven Bullaert and family

# Serene and Organic

Tucked away in Eksaarde, East Flanders, along the meandering Moervaart, a long, gabled farmhouse defies rigid lines. A study in roundness, the adobe structure carries the same sculptural appeal as César Manrique's Mirador del Río on Lanzarote. Constructed around on a wooden skeleton, its walls were given a new skin of lime, hemp, and woven willow branches. A clever consequence of this combination is natural climate control; the house stays warm in winter and cool in summer. For artist and product developer Sven Bullaert, Casa UMU is more than a residence. It is the embodiment of his holistic vision of living and personal foundation: stillness and art, a place to feel, reflect, and create. Here, Belgian minimalism meets southern warmth, free of sharp angles and rich in rustic elements. As the former creative director of Kipling, his work has taken him across continents. Observing communal living in Asia and Africa, he found inspiration in the bond between spaces and the people who inhabit them. Seeking a place in which to recharge, experiment, and connect, he took a leap and moved here with his wife and three children. Over the course of a decade, they immersed themselves in the rhythms of nature, molding their philosophy of home, one season at a time. The living room is now housed in the former stable, preserving its original volume. The suspended fireplace takes center stage in the sunken lounge, a nod to the 1970s, framed by a softly patinated, cognac leather Togo sofa set by Michel Ducaroy for Ligne Roset and an inviting Eames lounge chair. Light pours in from every angle, thanks to Bullaert's use of geometric windows to outline nature and create a dialogue between the landscape and beyond. Terra-cotta tones alternate with burgundy and turquoise touches, whether in a high-pile rug or a textured pillow. Bullaert's sfumato paintings, soft-edged and abstract, grace the walls, subtly expanding the dimensions of each room. The showpiece? The music room, featuring sublime Synthese speakers—an innovation the designer first worked on during his studies in the 1980s.

Synesthesia shapes Bullaert's design language, guiding him to curved, organic forms. What moves him most at Casa UMU is how light flows through its spaces from dawn to dusk—a humbling reminder of our place within the elements, the universe.

Each flattened stone was placed into the floor with meticulous precision. What fills the home is equally intentional: soulful objects from Africa and artworks by Bullaert himself—each one chosen for presence, not just aesthetics.

Martin

Former Tin Can Factory, Bruges. *Designed by* Frieda Degeyter.
*Inhabited by* Frieda Degeyter and Vincent Plasschaert

# Industrial Turned Vintage

Sometimes plan B—plan Bruges, in this case—turns out better than plan A, which for Frieda Degeyter had been Antwerp. Drawn to its artistic pulse, the fashion designer and stylist had fallen for the city after graduating from its academy. But everything shifted when her partner Vincent Plasschaert, owner of a timber company, stumbled upon a former tin can factory in Bruges, split into rooftop units for sale. The couple claimed three sections and a garden—for a fraction of what it would have cost in Antwerp. Degeyter and Plasschaert were set on maintaining the building's industrial soul. They sanded and repainted the original roof structure with its metal support beams, and they salvaged an oversized extractor hood from the factory, placing it above the kitchen island. Two large niches by the seating area once served as access gates. For privacy, the couple tucked the bathroom and front-facing bedrooms into a separate enclosed section. In the case of the interior, Plasschaert gave Degeyter complete control—no questions asked. And who could blame him? The daughter of anarchitect, Degeyter grew up surrounded by the likes of Aalto, Eames, and Jacobsen—design was practically served with her cereal. It shows. Walk through the space and you will spot iconic furniture at every turn: Bertoia bar stools, Eames office chairs, and an oval Saarinen Tulip table surrounded by matching chairs—the latter scooped up many years ago, for just a few hundred euros. All preloved, they have been collected over time and represent a lifelong passion for Degeyter that stands in quiet defiance of the status-symbol weight vintage design tends to carry today. It is a sensibility that also finds its way into her fashion practice, where she takes an active stand against fleeting trends. Her rebellious energy—flowing through both her work and her interior—reveals a desire for clash amid beauty. Tension is welcome, just look at the almost hysterical multicolored synthetic wig lamp on the low console table, or the low-slung, eye-catching fireplace mid space. Clashing, collecting, rethinking—proof that Belgian homes do not have to play it safe to be timeless.

The striking white, angular desk, designed by Degeyter's mother for her father, is a true one-off—a family heirloom. Further into the loft, three rows of round paper lamps float in midair, like a cluster of balloons.

In the lounge, chocolate-brown carpet stretches across the floor and walls, exuding a 1970s feel—by evening, it evokes the mood of a snazzy hotel lobby. A sofa in the very same shade hosts a parade of pillows—no two alike—as if trying to swallow the piece whole.

# Creative Homes

## Interiors and Design in Belgium

This book was conceived, edited, and designed by gestalten.

Edited by Robert Klanten and François-Luc Giraldeau
With Contributing Editor Living Inside Ltd.

Photography by Luc Roymans
Text by Sanne Bolten

Editorial management by Anna Diekmann
Design, Cover, and Layout by Stefan Morgner
Photo editing by Madeline Dudley-Yates
Production management by Martin Bretschneider

Typefaces by Reto Moser (GT Alpina) and Bureau Brut (Droulers Clarendon)



Printed by Grafisches Centrum Cuno GmbH & Co. KG, Calbe (Saale)
Made in Germany

Published by gestalten, Berlin 2025
ISBN 978-3-96704-189-7

1st printing, 2025



For more information, and to order books, please visit www.gestalten.com

Die Gestalten Verlag GmbH & Co. KG
Mariannenstrasse 9–10
10999 Berlin, Germany
hello@gestalten.com

Bibliographic information published by the Deutsche Nationalbibliothek.
The Deutsche Nationalbibliothek lists this publication in the Deutsche Nationalbibliografie; detailed bibliographic data is available online at www.dnb.de

None of the content in this book was published in exchange for payment by commercial parties or designers; gestalten selected all included work based solely on its artistic merit.

This book was printed on paper certified according to the standards of the FSC®.